How to Start a Catering Business When You Don't Know What the *Hell* You're Doing

A Practical Guide for Aspiring Caterers Who Lack Professional Training

Written By

Jennifer Williams

ISBN: 1-4033-5889-3 (e-book)
ISBN: 1-4033-5890-7 (Paperback)

Library of Congress Control Number: 2002093555

This book is printed on acid free paper.

Printed in United States of America
Bloomington, IN

1stBooks – rev. 10/24/02

I dedicate this book to my husband Vernon for loving and

supporting me in all that I do.

And to my mom and dad for encouraging me to live my dreams.

Introduction

It's not easy to admit that you don't know what the hell you are doing, but I felt that it was time someone fess up to it, especially when it comes to catering. I have spoken to many people who would love to start a catering business but they are intimidated by the "master chefs" of the world and are afraid to try it on their own. Lots of these people have even completed professional training and are still wondering if they are good enough.

Catering is art, and just like any other type of art, it takes passion. If you are passionate about cooking, then you already possess the main component to being a great caterer. Running the business requires other skills and I am hoping that this book will help those who lack those gifts. I do not profess to be a fabulous caterer or even an extraordinary chef. I simply love to cook and I found a way to make money doing what I love - and you can too. I wanted to share my experiences, my knowledge, and my mistakes with you to help you get started. There are lots of other books out there that can help you once you get established, but I never found one written by someone that started from scratch and who lacked professional training. I never found a book written by someone that would admit they didn't know what the hell they were doing.

Chapter One

How I Got Started

Jennifer Williams

I have always loved to cook. I spent countless hours as a kid in the kitchen with my mom, who is a fabulous cook, helping with holiday feasts, Christmas baking and Sunday dinners. I baked my first piecrust from scratch when I was 8 years old. I used to tell my parents, "I want to own a restaurant when I grow up." I also wanted to be a veterinarian, a lawyer and an actress, but that's another book.

One day, shortly after my 29th birthday my mom called me and told me about a little café that was for sale where she and her friends eat lunch. She wondered if I was interested in buying it. Without thinking for more than 5 seconds I said "YES" and two months later I was standing in the café kitchen at 5am preparing to open for the first time thinking "What the hell am I doing?" I had never really worked in a restaurant before except for a deli when I was in high school. And I had never run one.

The previous owner had served things like tuna salad on biscuits, beef jerky and gravy poured over everything. I changed the menu immediately and began creating my own signature sandwiches and homemade soups. To my amazement and delight, customers came in and liked what they ate. I even had my own "regulars" that came in everyday for lunch and chitchat. I was truly a restauranteer—or so I thought.

The restaurant business is a tough business. I once met a man on an airplane and he asked me what I did for a living. I excitedly told him that I was in the restaurant business. He too was in the business and he spent the next two hours bursting my balloon by telling me how I was never going to make it if I only served breakfast and lunch. He said that there would be a time when I would have to find other ways to make money with the business. He was right. I was having a hard time paying my bills and making ends meet and just like the man had warned, I needed to find a way to make extra income with my little café if I wanted to stay in business.

One of my regular customers put the idea of catering in my head when she approached me one day and asked if I catered. Without hesitation I said "of course", and before I knew it I had booked my very first catering job.

Some of you may be thinking that I had an advantage over home-based caterers because I had a restaurant, but I don't see it that way. That first job was the only job that came to me without me initiating the meeting. I worked very hard to get every job I booked in the beginning until referrals starting coming in. Once I catered that first job, I knew I wanted to cater full time so I worked hard and built my catering business from nothing to over twenty jobs my first year. My second year I booked thirty jobs.

Catering is really hard work but if you love what you are doing, you won't mind the blisters on your feet, the long hours and the constant smell of onion and garlic on your fingers. I know I don't!

Jennifer Williams

Chapter 2

Getting Legal

Jennifer Williams

Starting a new business does not require a degree in business but you will need to do some legal stuff to get yourself up and running. I have listed the steps that I went through to open my catering business but you should check with your local agencies to make sure procedures in your area are the same.

The first thing you should do is a file a Fictitious Name with the county clerks office. This is where you register your company name if you are using a name other than your own. You will check the county records to see if anyone else in the county is using the company name you have chosen and you will pay a fee. You will need to do this before you apply for a business license.

Next you will need to get your business license. If you are opening a business within the city limits you will apply for your license at the city office. If you are outside of the city limits, you will apply at the county. There is a fee to file. Most states base the fee on your projected annual sales. Renewal fees are based on your actual sales. You will need a business license if you plan to open a checking account using your company name.

You will also need to contact the IRS regarding self-employment taxes. Everyone must pay Social Security tax, even if you are self-employed. Contact the IRS at 800-829-1040 for more information.

You may also need a Health Permit. This is the worst part of the process or at least I found it to be. You will apply for the Permit at the County Office and they will assign you an agent. Every state is different so I strongly urge you to call your local county office to find out their rules and regulations.

In the state of California the requirements are very strict. To open a catering business all food must be prepared in a Health Approved kitchen that has been inspected by your assigned agent. They will then come out every year unannounced to check on you. If you are working from your home you can rent a kitchen from a local restaurant or bakery and use their permit, or you can try and get your home kitchen approved. I know lots of caterers that have chosen to not contact the Health Department. If you choose to go this route you have to be careful about how you advertise or you could get an unwanted visitor.

I must, at this point, tell you about my ugly run-in with my Health Inspector. I had only been in business a year and I had already had three visits from my assigned inspector. She was young, pregnant, and extremely rude. She would always come at lunchtime when my shop was the busiest, and then proceed to nag me about the bleach content in my mop bucket or the PH balance of my dishwater. She wouldn't leave until she could write me up for at least one item. This was the day that I decided I had had enough.

I asked her why she seemed to take joy in making it hard for me to conduct business and I would appreciate if she could drop by at a different time other than lunchtime. She proceeded to tell me that she could come anytime she liked and that she could make things even harder for me. It was at that moment that something in me snapped. I felt an anger that I had never experienced before or since. I was standing on one side of the counter and she was standing on the other side. My employees were standing next to me, staring at me, waiting to hear my response. They had never seen me angry or upset. Within seconds, I was lunging over the counter with my hands extended, reaching for her throat. George, one of my employees, grabbed the back of my shirt and pulled me off the counter. I was screaming like a mad woman for her to get the @&*@ out of my shop. Looking quite frightened, she ran out to her car. I wanted to run after her but George was still holding onto my shirt collar and I couldn't break free.

After regaining my composure and assuring everyone that I had not gone off the deep end, I called the Health Department office and demanded that she be fired or reprimanded for her threats against me. She of course denied the entire incident but I was assigned a different inspector. The best part—I didn't have another inspection for nearly two years. Although I am not proud of my behavior, this woman drove me literally nuts. Now you understand why I tell you at the beginning of this section that getting a Health Permit was the worst part of the process for me.

Before you apply for any licenses I recommend you contact the SBA—Small Business Administration. I couldn't believe a government agency could be so helpful. I found them so helpful that I have listed each states local office phone number for you in the back of this book. You can also visit them at www.sba.gov or call the SBA Answer Desk 800-827-5722 or email to answerdesk@sba.gov. They have a business plan tutorial that I highly recommend checking out. They teach you how to write a loan proposal and tell you about loan programs. The SBA offers training seminars and counseling help as well as telling you what agencies you need to contact before opening your business. Their Women's Business Center offers financing and business training that promotes the growth of women-owned businesses. They are a wealth of information for the small business owner.

Jennifer Williams

Chapter 3

Creating a User Friendly Menu

Jennifer Williams

Once you have decided to start catering you will need to create a menu. I had collected sample menus from other caterers but a lot of the food I had never eaten, let alone prepared. You must create a menu that you feel comfortable with. My advice to you is "KEEP IT SIMPLE". Create your menu around the type of clientele you attract. I found myself catering for a lot of retreat groups and corporate functions so I created a menu that could be set-up buffet style; dishes that are elegant but simple.

Although it is nice to show off some of your "fancier" dishes, many people are afraid to try new things so be sure to include some old simple favorites such as Baked Chicken, Meatloaf, or Lasagna. You should also keep in mind that too many choices can overwhelm your prospective client so limit your menu to 10-15 entrees. Inform your prospective client that you would be happy to prepare something special if they don't see it on the menu.

Never put a dish on your menu that you have never prepared. I once put Chicken Marsala on my menu thinking it would be a nice change from the other pasta dishes I normally prepare, but I had never tried out a recipe. The recipe I did have was not correct in its measurements so the sauce was terrible. At the last minute, I was re-creating a Marsala Sauce from a recipe I pulled from the Internet. I wasted a lot of time and money because I had not done my homework.

Here is a sample of my buffet menu:

Herb Baked Chicken (Everyone's favorite)

Marinated Tri-Tip

Poached Salmon

Meatloaf

Chicken Cordon Bleu

Teriyaki Beef or Chicken

Prime Rib

Pasta with Marinara Sauce

Linguini with Clams

Baked Filet of Sole

Prime Rib

Side Dishes

Escalloped Potatoes

Whipped Yams

Mashed Potatoes

Rice Pilaf

Chive Buttered Carrots

Steamed Vegetables

Green Beans with Almonds

Garden or Caesar Salad

Don't be afraid to change your menu. Your regular customers will really appreciate it. In the summer remove some of the heavier entrees and add a couple of lighter more health conscience dishes such as salads and fish. Try new recipes and when you find one that you really like call it the "Featured Entrée" and offer it at a special per person price to get customers to try it. It's nice to see people order something other than the Baked Chicken.

Jennifer Williams

Chapter 4

How Much Do I Charge These People?

Jennifer Williams

One of the hardest things to do when you are just starting out is how to determine what you will charge for your services. I am about to share a secret with you that I have never shared before. I tried using all of those cost analysis formulas, I even bought a software program to help me but I still couldn't figure it out. I decided to call some of my catering competition and pose as a potential client (I did mention that I also wanted to be an actress!) I would ask them to send me a menu and price list or to price a particular event. Then, based on the size of their operation, I would adjust my prices accordingly. If they were a large operation I knew they had a lot more overhead than I did so I would lower my per person price. If they were small like me, I would keep it about the same price. Once you start doing more jobs you will get a feel for what the actual costs are, and I have included a form that I used to help me with cost analysis.

If you don't like my "theatrical approach" you can always call caterers outside of your area and tell them you are just starting out and could they please send you their sales package. I tried this and found that a few were receptive but most caterers seemed put-off and never sent me anything.

Remember that your time and talent is worth a lot. Don't sell yourself short and be sure to charge for your time. In addition to the price per person I charge my customers for my time as well as the time for any staff that I use.

The current rates local caterers are charging their clients:

On site chef	$30.00 - 35.00 per hour
Servers	$20.00 - 25.00 per hour
Bartenders	$25.00 per hour
Busboys	$15.00 per hour

The general rule of thumb when charging your client for staff is one (1) staff person for every 25 guests. So, if your client has 75 guests, you would need an on-site chef and three (3) servers plus any additional staff they have requested such as a bartender.

Chapter 5

Marketing Your Catering

Business

Jennifer Williams

Before you open your catering business you should decide what kind of customers you want to attract. I catered mostly for corporations so I didn't waste my time talking to people about weddings. I didn't want to do weddings, but a lot of caterers do business with anyone that needs a caterer. Whoever you decide to market to, know that market—what are the popular dishes being served at those kind of functions, get to know the venues so you know the set-ups, and have separate catering packets for each kind of business you will going after. You want to appear like you have done hundreds of jobs just like the one this customer is talking to you about, so do your homework!

Professional Organizations

How you market your catering business can make or break you. One of your best bets is to join a local professionals group such as the Chamber of Commerce or a Referrals Group. You may not be one for getting up at 6am to have breakfast in a business suit but you can make a lot of great contacts. I made the greatest contact of my catering career through the Chamber, which I discuss at the end of this chapter.

Most of the business people that join these professional organizations only do business with other members. I was the only caterer in my group and therefore got a lot of referrals. The dues are generally inexpensive to join these groups and it is money well spent. Contact your local Chamber of Commerce office or go to www.uschamber.com to find the office nearest you.

Community Events

Catering community events is a great way to get your name in front of people. I met with our local Police Department and volunteered to cater boxed lunches for their after school program once a month. Once the program took off they started paying me to do it every week. I also cater fund raising events, such as events for our local library and programs for the elderly. I hosted a food booth at our annual street fair and I have catered several pancake breakfasts for the Chamber of Commerce. Every event led to at least one other job and I got to be involved in the community. Look for events in your area where you can provide your talents. You'll be doing a service to the community and building your business in the process.

Newspaper

Another way to market your business is to call the business section of your local newspaper and request to be a featured business in an upcoming edition. When I did this I didn't know what to expect. The paper sent out a photographer that took several photos of me and my staff preparing for a job, as well as interviewing me. What I thought would be a small blurb turned out to be a two full pages with a large article and several photographs. I got 15 jobs from that article and I didn't have to pay a penny for it.

Internet

I recently read that approximately 65% of caterers out there have a website to advertise their business. It is no secret that the Internet is a very important business tool and more people are using it than ever. But does that mean you need to build website? Not necessarily right away but I do recommend it once you are established. It is a great way for prospective clients to check you out before making contact with you.

I visited nearly 50 websites for caterers in my area and found that most of them posted their menus, had fabulous photos of their food, and had a way for prospective clients to reach them via email as well as listing their contact phone numbers. You should check out the types of sites your local caterers have built to get ideas. It has become fairly inexpensive to have someone build a basic site for you or you can use a software program like Publisher or FrontPage to help you build your own.

If you are not ready to build a site you can always advertise on someone else's such as the LCA—Leading Caterers of America. They have a wonderful website designed to help prospective clients find caters in their area. It is an awesome site, very easy to use, and there is no charge to register your company and no charge for referrals. They also have some very helpful articles and loads of advice for the new caterer. Visit them at www.leadingcaterers.com and see for yourself.

Client Referrals

One of the best advertisements for your business is a satisfied customer. All caters rely heavily on referrals to get business. I would recommend getting some business cards printed right away and give several to each of your customers. You could offer them a discount on their next catered event if they refer a friend. Whenever I book a job based on a referral I always send a thank you card to the customer with some more of my cards.

Vendor Referrals

Another source of referrals that is often overlooked are vendor referrals. Florists, photographers and D.J's are an excellent source of referrals but are often overlooked by the caterer. My husband is a wedding photographer and he always says that he only refers caters that feed him at events. It may sound silly but most photographers or DJ's have been working for several hours without a meal. Even if your client does not want to pay for vendor meals, it is in your best interest to make sure these people are well fed. They come in contact with many people asking for a good caterer. Do you think they'll remember your name if you refused to feed them? I doubt it.

Since you don't usually have the opportunity to feed the florist or wedding coordinator, plan to drop off muffins or cookies at his/her shop or office and leave some of your cards. Catering is all about relationships. Not just with your customers but other professionals that can help you grow your business and reputation.

Advertising

I have one simple sentence for you - **Do not place an ad in the Yellow Pages.** It is very expensive and for caterers it is one of the most useless advertising tools out there. I placed an ad that cost me 300.00 per month and in 2 years I received 5 calls and zero jobs from the ad. In speaking to other caterers in the area they agreed with me that there is very little return for them. The only caterers that have large ads in the phone book are caterers that are already established. They advertise in the yellow pages to show their stability in the industry, not to get new business.

You can list you name for a nominal fee if you choose but I would recommend spending the money in other areas that are proven ways to increase your business.

Printed Materials

As I mentioned before, one of the first things you should do is get business cards printed. You can print them yourself from your computer but I recommend having a printer do them. It's not very expensive and they look more professional. The other printed items I recommend ordering are letterhead for printing quotations and invoices, and a menu. You will want to assemble a sales packet for prospective clients and it should contain the following items:

♦ **Business Cards**

♦ **Menu**—you can print this onto your letterhead.

♦ **References**—as you build your business list the jobs you have successfully done. Before listing anyone's name or phone number be sure to ask if you can use them.

♦ **Any write—ups** you may have received in newspapers or magazines.

♦ **Price list**

♦ **Rental Equipment you offer**

Purchase some pocket folders and adhere a label with your name on the front. Carry these packets in your car and your briefcase. You never know when you'll run into someone who is looking for a caterer.

Networking that Paid Off

While attending one of many Chamber of Commerce functions, I met a woman who was the manager of a local hotel. She was scheduled to host a mixer and needed a caterer because her hotel did not offer food service other than breakfast. She wondered if I could do it for a reduced cost and in return I would co-host the event to publicize my own business. I agreed and the event was a huge success for both of us.

After the mixer, we discussed her dilemma of not being able to rent her meeting rooms as often as she would like because most of the groups wanted meal service and she was unable to do that for them. The solution to her problem WAS ME! Whenever a group approached her about renting a meeting room and needing food service, she gave them my name and catering package. She would tell the customer that I was the Official Caterer for the hotel and I would handle all of their food related needs. In dealing with the customers directly, I felt comfortable that all the details would be taken care of and nothing would fall through the cracks.

The clients paid me directly for the food and paid the hotel for the room. The hotel saw an enormous jump in meeting room bookings and I was catering nearly every weekend for them.

I highly recommend getting a hold of hotels in your area to find out which ones don't offer food service. Set up an appointment with the manager and see if they will recommend you to their clients. Be persistent and take catering packets, business cards, and food samples frequently. You will be shocked at the amount of business just one hotel can bring to you.

I provided boxed lunches and deli platters as well as buffet and sit-down dinners. And remember, don't rule them out because they serve breakfast. For most hotels, that is the only food service they provide. Some hotels will even let you use their kitchen.

Jennifer Williams

Chapter 6

Close the Deal & Get Your Money

Jennifer Williams

You've shown them your menu, you've quoted the job, now it's time to close the deal. If they seem to be hesitating, ask them if they have any questions. Address any concerns they may have and then set the date.

Once they have agreed to use you, **GET A DEPOSIT!** Don't let them leave without giving you a check for at least a 25% deposit of the total job. I would recommend getting 50% up front to hold the date and collecting the balance one week prior to the event. That way all of your costs are covered in case the event is cancelled last minute. You will need to create a **Cancellation and Refund Policy** as well as a **Contract** for your customer to sign. I have enclosed a copy of my policy and contract at the end of this book. Feel free to copy and use it.

A contract is very important because it will protect you in case your client cancels last minute and demands their deposit back. This is especially important if you have already purchased food for the event. You can always work with a client allowing them to book another date with the deposit or you can refund the portion that wasn't used for supplies It is entirely up to you, as long as you have the signed contract.

Plan on contacting your client the week prior to the event to answer any questions they may have. Go over the details of the set-up and secure the time that you will show-up. If you haven't collected the balance due prior to the event, be sure to get it before the guests arrive.

Chapter 7

How Much Do I Serve?

Portion Sizes

Jennifer Williams

When I was starting out I spent countless hours at the bookstore and library trying to find a book that would tell me "this amount of food will feed this amount of people". I never found one, so I came up with my own system. I am sure that a more experienced caterer would laugh at my system, but it worked well and left me with little wasted food.

When you're serving beef or pork and the crowd is a combination of men and women you should figure ½ lb. of meat per person. If it is just women you may want to figure ¼ lb per person if you have several side dishes. If you only have a salad and rolls I would stick to the ½ lb rule.

Chicken is a little trickier. If it is just breast meat I always figure that half the group will come back for seconds so if I was serving 50 people I would prepare 75 breasts. If you are serving breasts, legs and thighs, figure 2 pieces per person.

When preparing your side dishes you should figure ¾ cup of potatoes or rice and 1 cup of vegetables per person. If you are using pre-packaged potatoes or canned vegetables you can feel safe following the serving guidelines listed on the box or can. For salads I would prepare about 1 cup of salad per person if it is a side dish. Prepare 2 cups per person if it is the main meal. I find that only about ¼ of the group will come back for seconds.

You will get a feel for portions as you do more jobs but I found these guidelines very helpful and I hope you do too.

Portion sizes goes against everything my mother (and probably yours) ever taught me. When my mom made food for 4 that meant food for 8. For Thanksgiving we could have fed the entire neighborhood. Her worst fear was running out of food. But remember, when you are catering, you want to run out of food after everyone has had an adequate meal. That means more money in your pocket at the end of the day and a lot less waste.

Chapter 8

What to Do with Leftover Food

Jennifer Williams

In the beginning you will probably have some leftover food until you get comfortable with portion sizes. Your client may request that you send the leftovers home with them. It is in your best interest if you have a policy of NOT sending leftovers home unless the food:

1. Doesn't need to be reheated

2. Will not spoil without refrigeration

If a person takes home chicken and leaves it in their car overnight and then eats in the morning and gets sick, you can bet they will somehow try to blame you. If they are dumb enough to eat it they are too dumb to figure out that you were not to blame. The only items I send home are desserts, crudités and cold appetizers.

If you find that you have a lot of leftover crudité (vegetable platter) consider taking it home and cutting it up for another job. I use it in sauces and salads. If I have leftover tri-tip I may use it in Enchiladas or for sandwiches. (Great if you have a sandwich route - see other types of catering)

Jennifer Williams

Chapter 9

What to Buy? Staples &

Equipment

Jennifer Williams

When you land your first job your initial response is to go out and purchase all kinds of catering equipment and supplies. In this chapter I will hopefully save you some money and help you figure out exactly what you will need on every job.

The first pieces I purchased were 3 chafers. You will use them on nearly every job and they will pay for themselves almost immediately. I would recommend purchasing simple, non-decorative chafers and hotel pans at a restaurant supply or Smart and Final (smartandfinal.com) which is where I purchased mine for around $75 each. They usually come with full sized hotel pans so I would recommend purchasing a few half pans for your side dishes and sauces. I tried using the disposable pans in the beginning and found them to be great for clean up but they were very flimsy. They would start falling into the water about halfway through the buffet line.

You will also want to purchase serving spoons, tongs and serving forks. I got some great ones at Ikea for about $3 each. Be sure to get a few large slotted spoons as well. Another piece of equipment that you may want to consider purchasing is a coffee urn. You will need it at nearly every job and they are around $20 to rent. I purchased mine used from a restaurant supply for $100. I also purchased hot pots, which keeps coffee and tea water hot and fresh for about 10 hours. They are great if you are catering at a place without electrical outlets.

You will need baskets in a variety of shapes and sizes. I use baskets for bread, silverware, napkins, condiments and decoration. Search thrift stores and swap meets first before heading to a retail store. Baskets can be expensive but they don't have to be. Another item to search for is salt and pepper shakers. You will need them on every job and I bought 10 sets so I could place them on every table. Not all the sets need to match but if you want new ones look at Smart and Final.

I recommend purchasing 6 or 7 plastic storage bins to store and transport your supplies. They're a great way to keep all of your stuff together at home and at the job. Below is a list of staples that I keep in my bins at all times. You should inventory the items before another job and keep it stocked.

> **Butter packets** - *you will keep in frig*
>
> **Sugar packets** - *pink, blue and regular*
>
> **Salt and Pepper**

Tabasco

Ketchup - *some people eat it on everything*

Toothpicks

Carry out containers

Trash bags

Sponges

Paper towels

Bar rags

Extra plates and napkins

Styrofoam or paper cups

Matches/ lighters

Lemons - *I cut into wedges at job*

Coffee stirrers

Aspirin

Band-aids

Sanitary napkins

You may find some of the items on my list unusual but I came up with my list based on customer requests. If you have a customer ask for something at a job, write it down. You may want to add it to your list.

Jennifer Williams

Chapter 10

Catering Do's & Don'ts

Jennifer Williams

The Do's:

Bring trash bags, sponges, bar towels—everything you will need to clean up after the event. You may find the hostess has had a bit too much to drink by the end of the night and is in no condition to point out where she keeps her cleaning supplies.

Do:

Bring Styrofoam or paper coffee cups to every party. Even if the client tells you she will provide them, bring some just in case. I have had several jobs where they forgot to get them and we ended up using her personal mugs for coffee service. Not only did we run out of mugs but we had more dishes to wash at the end of the evening.

Do:

Arrive 3-4 hours before the party is scheduled to start. This gives you ample time to start cooking, get the table set and acquaint yourself with a strange kitchen.

Do:

Have your staff/bartenders arrive 1 hour before the start of the party. Utilize them to help you get the bar set-up, the serving trays ready, crudité prepared and to brief them on the party details. Be sure to introduce them to your client.

Do:

Seek out your client and their spouse throughout the party offering them the first taste of everything you are serving. You want them to be well fed and you will want their feedback on the dishes you have prepared.

Do:

Wear a chef's coat and if necessary, pull you hair back. Ask your staff to wear similar clothing such as black slacks and white tuxedo shirts. It looks much more professional and distinguishes you from the guests. Remember, your staff's appearance reflects directly onto you so don't be afraid to send someone home to change if they are dressed inappropriately. You may want to pack an extra shirt or slacks with you just in case.

Do:

Ask you client if you can set-up a table or partition to discourage guests from entering the kitchen during the event. You would be surprised at the number of people that will come into the kitchen and start eating food right off the trays or snooping in the refrigerator while you are trying to work. The last thing you want while you are stuffing 100 mushrooms is some guy hanging around fingering all of the food and asking if you are married or single. I speak from experience!

Do:

Send your client a thank you card no later than a week following the party. Be sure to include some of your business cards.

Do:

Drink plenty of water. It will help you stay alert and focused. It will also help keep a headache from forming due to dehydration.

Do:

Have a nibble of food away from the guests or before the party starts. Passing out from low blood sugar is NOT ALLOWED!

Do:

Wear comfortable shoes. This is not the time to break in your new pair of loafers.

Do:

Have a "debriefing" meeting with your staff within 3 days of the party. Get your staff's feedback on the details of the event while it is still fresh in their minds. You would be surprised what you miss while you are stuck in the kitchen all night. Go over any problems, pat each other on the back, and discuss any upcoming jobs.

Do:

Re-wash your hands in the kitchen after coming out of the bathroom. I once witnessed a guest and a staff person arguing because the guest didn't believe the server washed her hands after using the bathroom. Since then, I have made a habit of always washing my hands where anyone who cares can see me do it. Then there is no question regarding my personal hygiene and food handling.

Do:

Be certain your client has paid you the final bill before you leave. I recommend you get your money before the guests arrive and the champagne starts flowing.

Do:

Take plenty of business cards with you and have them ready to give out. Give some to each of your staff as well.

Do:

Have a great time!!!

The Don'ts

Drink alcohol before or during the party. Never give your customer ammunition against you in case something goes wrong.

Don't:

Park in the driveway. Once you have unpacked your car, move it away from the house. Also inform your staff.

Don't:

Eat in front of the guests. Its looks tacky if they ask for your business card and your mouth is full of food.

Don't:

Be afraid to look in cupboards for things you need before bothering your client. She will most likely appreciate your initiative. I would recommend however that you ask your client if there are things that she would prefer you not use, and then inform your staff.

Don't:

Wear lots of makeup and cologne. It is inappropriate and you want the guests to smell the food, not you.

Don't:

Lose your cool in front of the guests if things go wrong. If you run into a problem, handle it like a professional. No cussing or throwing utensils! Only involve your client if you absolutely can't handle it yourself.

Don't:

Answer your cell phone unless it is an emergency. You are being paid to work, not book other jobs on your client's time.

Don't:

Reprimand staff in front of your client or the guests. It's humiliating for the employee and makes you look bad. Save it for after the party.

Chapter 11

Hiring & Paying Staff

Jennifer Williams

The best place to find staff for your catering business is restaurants or other caterers. Most waiters/waitresses and bartenders take jobs on the side and will be happy to make some extra money working for you. Call around to other caterers in the area and see if they have someone they work with that they would be willing to send your way. Or, the next time you eat out, if you have a waitperson that you really like, see if they would be interested in making some extra money working for you.

You've hired them, so now you have to pay them. I paid my catering staff in cash but sent them a 1099 at the end of the year. This way I didn't have to pay employment taxes but I could still write off the salaries I paid them. If you choose to have a payroll, you will have to contact the IRS to get an Employer's ID Tax Number. You will also need to contact your state office. There are a lot of expenses associated with payroll, so be certain this is the way you want to do it before you start the process.

Some caterers just pay their staff in cash and that's the end of it. Whichever way you plan to pay your staff you will want to discuss it with them prior to bringing them aboard. It will avoid problems later.

I don't recommend hiring family members or friends. When I first went into business, I hired my sister-in-law to help me out. Although we worked fine together, my brother had issues with it and eventually it led to me and her having problems that could only be solved by her not working with me. It is sometimes hard for those who love you to see you as anything other than sister, daughter, or friend and not as BOSS. I am not saying that you should never use anyone you know. Sometimes you will be in a bind and really need someone to fill in. I just wouldn't rely on them as your only staff.

It's nice if you can find a couple of people that will work for you on a regular basis. You learn each other's work habits, strengths and weaknesses, and ultimately you work better together. You will want to work with people that take instruction well and that you can rely on. There is nothing worse than having a staff person, like the bartender, not show up. This is why I always say that although you want to build a relationship with your staff, don't ever forget that you are the boss. If you become their close friend, some people will take advantage of you. You just want to be careful whom you hire.

Don't ever do what I did and hire out of desperation. I ended up with a guy that nearly cost me one of my biggest clients because he showed up to the event slightly drunk and looking very sweaty and gross. My dad was able to step in and man the barbeque and save my butt, but this wouldn't have happened if I had followed my instincts and not hired him at all.

Trust your instincts! That's my final answer.

Jennifer Williams

Chapter 12

Getting Technical

Jennifer Williams

Okay, here's your big chance to use your computer for more than playing solitaire and e-mailing silly jokes to your friends (sorry Mom)!

There are some wonderful software programs on the market to help you manage your catering business. I checked out a couple of free demos when I first started the business but I never purchased a program. I have recently started looking at them again. Below, I have listed the programs that I found the most interesting and useful.

Caterware   800-853-1017

This is the ultimate catering software. It can manage every aspect of your business. It offers features such as billing, contact tracking, event calendar, and job costing. It also provides reports and will generate letters and envelopes. It provides e-mail and integrates with Microsoft Word and Office. This is not for the part-time caterer but is worth checking out. You can download a free demo from their website at www.caterware.com or call for a diskette.

Cater Pro Software 800-606-1597

Offers many of the same features as Caterware. Price includes 1 year of technical support which is really nice. Another nice feature is if you download their demo it will allow you to enter up to 15 actual catering events. This gives you the opportunity to use it on real clients. After the 15th event, you must purchase the software if you wish to continue using it. Visit their user - friendly and informative website at www.caterprosoftware.com

Costguard   888-325-6937

This software is specifically designed for food costing, pricing, inventory, recipe management, and menu costing. You can buy only modules that you need and they have bundled the most popular modules together at a special price.   Request a demo diskette at www.costguard.com.

Even if you can't afford one of the catering programs, I do recommend that you purchase an accounting program such as QuickBooks as soon as possible. In addition to keeping your accounts payable and receivables organized, QuickBooks will generate professional looking invoices and proposals. You get a lot for your money and it is user friendly.

You may also want to purchase a client contact program such as Goldmine or Outlook to manage your appointments and client information.

Another great item to consider purchasing is a PDA (Personal Data Assistant) such as the Palm Pilot. It eliminates jotting down phone numbers on cocktail napkins and gives you access to your clients information when you are out and about. You can even download software directly from the Internet.

Jennifer Williams

Chapter 13

Renting Stuff

You should look to build a relationship with a local rental company. They will become very important to you as you grow and get fancier jobs. They are the place you call when your customer needs china, glassware, tables and bars; items that you don't want to purchase and probably don't have the room to store. When you work with the same company for a while they will sometimes give you price breaks for being a regular customer.

You will bill your clients direct for the cost of rented equipment. I charge my clients 15% over my cost for all rentals plus delivery. It will be up to you to coordinate with the rental company when to deliver the items and when to pick them up. Some of your clients will rent items on their own but you may want to offer it as a service. It's an easy way to add some money to your profit margin.

If you are planning to include a rental sheet in your catering packet, you will definitely want to include the following items:

Banquet Tables

Round Tables—48" and 60"

Round Cocktail Tables—36"

Chairs—folding and stacking

Linens—napkins, tablecloths and skirting for buffet tables

Bars—4ft. and/or 6 ft.

Chapter 14

Should I Sell the VW

& Get a Van?

Jennifer Williams

Unless you were already planning to purchase a van, I would say don't spend the money. My catering mobile was a Honda Del Sol, two-seater, sport car, but boy did it have a huge trunk. I could fit two chafers with their lids and several bags of supplies. I would borrow my dad's truck for larger jobs, and my staff's cars were always recruited for transporting junk from job to job.

If you don't have a car suitable for catering and you can't borrow one from a friend or family member, you can always rent one. It's a lot cheaper than purchasing one and you can write the expense off on your taxes. The money would be much better spent promoting your growing business.

Whatever you drive, I would recommend getting advertising magnets for the side of your vehicle. It is an inexpensive advertising tool and gives you a more professional look when you drive up to a job site. You can purchase them from any office supply store. You should expect to pay about $50.00 per set.

Jennifer Williams

Chapter 15

Other Types Of Catering

Jennifer Williams

If the jobs aren't coming in as fast as you'd like them too, you may want to consider one of these ideas to get the money rolling and your business name out there.

I started a sandwich delivery business. In the morning I would prepare fresh sandwiches (roast beef, tuna, turkey, ham, vegetarian) and sell them to local businesses. I would keep them in a cooler in my car and when I stopped at a business park I would arrange them in basket, add a couple of muffins, cookies and bags of chips and go in smiling!

I printed up menus so that they could order for the next day. I told customers that they had to call or fax their orders before 10am for specialty items or they could just buy whatever I had in my basket that day. It didn't take long for my route to become popular. After about 3 weeks, I was making $100-$150 per day. Eventually I had my parents-in-law, who are retired, start another route. Before too long they were making $800-$1000 per week

In some business parks you will be competing with the catering trucks but I never found that to be a problem.

My route was successful because we appealed to the people in the offices who were looking for healthier items such as fresh sandwiches and salads. We came by at the same time every morning before they had a chance to decide on something else for lunch. Our stuff was different, such as turkey breast with cranberry in a pita.

Look for business parks that are out and away from restaurants. Most of the people that work in those offices are desperate for something better than they brought from home.

You will want to pack an assortment of water and sodas as well as baked goods and muffins. I bought all of my baked items and drinks from Costco and Smart and Final.

Change the items that you bring out on a regular basis. This will guarantee repeat business and will keep your regular customers from getting bored. Ask them if there is anything they would like to see you make. I made up order forms so that we could take special orders for the following day.

The sandwich route is also a great way to get catering customers. I had several route customers who started ordering lunches for business meetings. One of my customers asked me to cater their open house.

That lead to their company BBQ for 300 people. Hand out your business card with every order and drop off a catering packet at each location. You never know who will need your services in the future. I have included a copy of my sandwich menu for you to copy and use.

Another idea is to focus on one or two items that are your specialties such as a dessert or sandwich and try to market it to private groceries, restaurants or mini-markets. I had a few of my sandwiches for sale in mini-markets and groceries. I would stock their coolers and charge them for whatever they sold. You can design an eye-catching label and remember that you must list the sandwiches ingredients somewhere on the label.

I recommend using a sturdy bread such as sourdough or rolls when preparing the sandwiches. This will add to the sandwiches shelf life and potentially make you more money. Just remember to only stock a few sandwiches because you will have to toss whatever they don't sell.

You should create an inventory sheet that lists what items you have left in each store and be certain to get the store managers signature on the form.

Another idea is to market your product to local restaurants and coffee houses. A friend of mine marketed her cheesecakes to several restaurants and soon became the source for all of their desserts. Be persistent and take lots of samples with you. Who could resist a delicious piece of lemon cheesecake or chocolate chip muffin?

Chapter 16

BBQ Tips

Jennifer Williams

Cooking Tips

A lot of my jobs consisted of large corporate BBQ's. I quickly learned how to prepare tri-tip for 250 people without spending 4 hours sweating over a grill. And it will be some of the best tri-tip your guests have ever had.

The night before the BBQ, rub the tri-tip roasts with salt, pepper or marinate in your favorite sauce. I always marinate a couple of the roasts in a teriyaki marinade. It is always a big hit but be sure to inform your guests that it has been marinated in case they have a food allergy. After the meat has been seasoned/marinated, place in cooking bags. A large bag will hold 3 or so roasts. If you have never prepared meat using a cooking bag, you are in for a real treat. I use one every Thanksgiving for the turkey but they also have a million other uses.

Add a tablespoon of flour to keep the bag from bursting, seal the bag and cut a couple of holes in bag with scissors. Place in a roasting pan and bake at 350 degrees for 1-1 1/2 hours. Remove from oven and immediately place the roasts in the refrigerator. Leave the roasts in the bags.

Your tri-tip roasts are cooked so they just need to be reheated on the BBQ grill for approximately 45 minutes on the day of the event. Keep turning the meat so it doesn't burn. The meat will be very tender and easy to cut and your customers will think you are the Master BBQ chef!

I have also been known to bake my chicken the night before until it is half cooked. This saves a lot of time and space on your BBQ and it gives me peace of mind that all of chicken I am serving is thoroughly cooked. Bake the chicken in disposable hotel pans. Bake until the chicken is just starting to brown. Remove from oven and cover with tin foil. Refrigerate overnight.

The BBQ Site

If you are barbequing in a place that does not offer refrigeration, be sure to bring A LOT of ice. In addition to keeping all of your meat and mayonnaise-based salads on ice, you will need ice to keep you beverages cold. Plan on having someone from your staff run for ice a couple of times during the event.

If you are serving cake for dessert, see if the baker can deliver to the BBQ site and have them arrive about an hour before you are ready to serve dessert. That way you don't have to worry about flies or bees getting into the icing and it will be easier to cut if it hasn't been sitting out in the heat for a few hours.

A few days before the event is to take place, go the site and take a notebook with you. Make notes regarding the set-up. I sometimes take a Polaroid camera with me if I want to be certain of the set-up for decorating purposes. Look for electrical outlets, refrigeration, sinks, and find out about trash receptacles. If you are not sure about the trash set-up and there is no one you can ask, plan on bringing some large trashcans and bags. Plan on bringing a couple of rolls of toilet paper. Somehow it is always your fault if the bathrooms runs out of paper.

Dress comfortably and if your client says it is okay for you to wear shorts, I would wear them! You can wear shorts and still look professional. Wear an apron to protect your clothes and to distinguish you from the guests. Be sure to be specific with your staff about what is acceptable to wear and what is not acceptable, like cut off shorts or halter tops.

If there are electrical outlets, you could even bring a fan or two. I used to do that all the time. It kept my staff and me from looking all sweaty and it helped to keep the food cool.

Chapter 17

Menu Ideas

Jennifer Williams

Theme Buffet Menus:

Seafood Buffet:

Green Salad

Seafood Salad

Oyster on half shell and crab legs

Salmon Cakes *

Baked Filet of Sole

Rice Pilaf

Fresh Vegetables

Rolls & butter

Mexican Buffet:

Sweet Corn and Red Pepper Salad

Green Salad

Cheese Enchiladas

Beef or Chicken Fajitas

Oven Roasted Tri-tip

Spanish Rice

Refried Beans

Chips/Salsa/Guacamole/Flour Tortillas

Flan

Italian Buffet:

Antipasto Salad

Pasta Salad

Fettuccini Alfredo *

Chicken Parmesan

Spaghetti with Meat Sauce

Rolls with Butter

Fresh Vegetables

Assorted mini desserts

Passed Hors D'Oeuvres:

Parmesan Crostinis

Spinach & Feta Rolls *

Deviled Eggs *

Turkey & Spinach Pinwheels

Crab Stuffed Mushrooms

Mini Quiche

Cocktail Egg Rolls

Crab Cakes

Grilled Chicken Skewers

Buffalo Chicken Wings

Ricotta Cheese Puffs *

Buffet Style Hors D'Oeuvres:

Sweet & Sour Meatballs

BBQ Meatballs

Baked Brie with Honey

Crudités with Dill Dip

Salmon Mousse on Cucumber Rounds

Assorted Finger Sandwiches

Fresh Seasonal Fruit Display

Domestic Cheese Display with Crackers

Hummus Bi Tahini served with Pita Triangles *

Salads:

Chicken, Shrimp or Tuna Pasta

Greek with Feta

Antipasto

Seafood Medley

Tossed Greens

Warm Spinach

Caesar Salad

Cobb Salad

Oriental Chicken Salad

Traditional Potato or Macaroni Salads

Chapter 18

Recipes

Jennifer Williams

Turkey Cranberry Pita

1 Large Pita

Turkey Breast

Cream Cheese

Cranberry Sauce

Leaf Lettuce

Sprouts

Tomato Slices

Mix softened cream cheese and cranberry sauce together then spread inside of pita. Stuff with turkey (4 oz), lettuce, sprouts and tomatoes. It was one of my customer's favorites. It is also great on a dark bread like Squaw or Pumpernickle.

Hot Roast Beef

6 oz Roast Beef

Large Green mild chili

Swiss Cheese

Mustard/Mayo

Melt Swiss cheese on top of chili and roast beef. I served this on a cheese onion roll but would taste great on simple onion roll or hoagie roll. So simple but so delicious!

Vegetarian Sandwich

Cream Cheese

Cucumber slices

Leaf lettuce

Shredded carrot

Red onion

Sprouts

Tomato

Spread cream cheese on a whole grain bread. Start with lettuce, followed by cucumber, tomato, onion, and shredded carrots topped with sprouts. Serve with a packet of Italian dressing.

Add turkey breast to this sandwich to spruce up and old favorite. Offering your customers something different than they could make at home is one of the keys to the sandwich route success. **So be creative!**

Catering Recipes

Salmon Cakes

> canned salmon (15 oz can will make 12-15 miniature
>
> cakes)
>
> 1-cup breadcrumbs
>
> 1 egg
>
> 1/4 onion
>
> salt & pepper

Heat shallow layer of oil in a skillet. Mix above ingredients in food processor until mixed into a paste. Form into tablespoon balls and place in oil. Flatten with spatula. Turn frequently, allowing each side to turn a gold brown. Drain on paper towels. Serve with a dill or sour cream based sauce.

Fettuccini Alfredo (makes 12 servings)

> 2 lbs. Fettuccini noodles
>
> 1 cup grated Parmesan cheese
>
> 1 1/3 cup light cream or sour cream
>
> 2 lb. sweet butter

2 egg yolks

Prepare noodles according to package. While noodles are cooking beat egg yolks lightly and add to cream. Melt butter. Drain noodles and place in a warm serving bowl. Pour egg and cream mixture over noodles along with butter and 2 cup of cheese. Toss noodles with a fork and spoon until well blended. Toss in balance of just prior to serving. Top with additional cheese if desired.

Spinach & Feta Rolls (makes 18)

2 tablespoons vegetable oil

2 onions finely chopped

10 oz frozen spinach thawed

2 teaspoons dried dill weed

4 oz. Feta cheese, crumbled

1 egg beaten

3 tablespoons sour cream

12 sheets filo pastry

2 cup butter, melted

Heat oil in saucepan over low heat. Add onions and cook until soft but not browned. Meanwhile, drain spinach well, then place in colander and press out as much water as possible. Stir spinach into onions and cook for 2 minutes longer. Stir in dill weed and cheese. Remove from heat; cool. Mix in egg and sour cream. Cover and refrigerate until cold. Preheat oven to 400F. Work with 2 sheets of filo at a time keeping other sheets covered with damp paper towels or plastic wrap to prevent drying. Brush 1 sheet with melted butter. Top with another sheet. Cut sheets crosswise into 3 strips.

Place spoonful of filling at 1 end of each strip. Tuck in sides and roll up. Brush ends with melted butter and press lightly to seal. Repeat with remaining sheets of pastry. Place rolls, seam down on baking sheets. Bake about 15 minutes or until golden brown. Serve hot.

Deviled Eggs (makes 24)

12 eggs

8 oz cream cheese

1-cup mayonnaise

dash of cayenne pepper (optional)

paprika

To ensure that your yolks will be centered, tightly pack in saucepan, pointed side facing down. Pour in enough cold water to cover and bring to a boil. Reduce heat, cover and simmer 10-15 minutes.

Drain eggs and rinse under cold water until cool enough to peel. Shell the eggs then cut each in half lengthwise. Place yolks, softened cream cheese, mayo and cayenne pepper in food processor or use hand mixer. When thoroughly mixed spoon mixture into a pastry bag with fluted top. Drain whites and pat dry before filling. Pipe yolk mixture into egg white and top with paprika.

Did you know that quick cooling your eggs will prevent a black ring from forming around the yolk?

Ricotta Cheese Puff (makes 20)

8 oz. Ricotta cheese

2 eggs

2 tablespoons all purpose flour

1-teaspoon salt

3 green onions chopped

1/4-cup parsley

2 teaspoons drain capers, coarsely chopped

Vegetable oil

In a bowl, beat cheese until smooth. Beat in eggs one at a time then add flour green onions, salt, capers and parsley. If you are not ready to cook, cover and refrigerate.

In a large skillet, heat 2 inches of oil to 350F. Drop teaspoons of cheese mixture into hot oil, a few at a time. Cook until golden brown on all side. Drain on paper towels and serve hot.

Hummus

2 cup dried garbanzo beans

2 teaspoons salt

4 garlic cloves

2 cup Tahini

lemon juice

1-tablespoon olive oil

Paprika

parsley whole

Pita bread cut into triangles

Rinse and sort beans. Soak overnight in cold water. Drain and place in a saucepan.

Add enough cold water to cover. Stir in salt. Bring to a boil; reduce heat, cover and simmer 2 hours or until beans are tender. Drain, saving the liquid. Place drained beans in food processor and process to make a smooth paste, adding a bit of saved liquid as needed. Add garlic, Tahini, and dash of lemon juice for taste. Process until blended. Place hummus into a serving bowl. Smooth the surface and drizzle with enough oil to keep from drying. Garnish with paprika and parsley.

Chapter 19

What the Hell Am I Doing Now?

Jennifer Williams

One of the hardest decisions I have ever had to make was to let go of my catering business. I had a baby after having had a very difficult pregnancy. The café business was terrible and I had to get rid of it. I wanted to keep catering since that is where I made most of my money, but with a new baby boy, it was just too difficult. I decided to take a break and focus on my son but I couldn't stop thinking about catering, so that's why I wrote this book. It's my way of staying in "the game".

We recently moved to a new area to be closer to my husbands work and I am preparing to start my sandwich route business again as a way to launch back into catering. I will also be talking to aspiring caterers about starting their own business so e-mail me if you would like a schedule of my upcoming seminars. Email me at Jenoffice1@aol.com for more information or just to chat about food and catering.

Now that I have had a catering business, the fear and mystery are gone. I know that I can do it again and make a success of it. I have already lived my dream once—now it's your turn!

Jennifer Williams

Chapter 20

Catering Forms

Jennifer Williams

Cost Worksheet cont'd

Customer _____

Date of Event _____Time

_____

Contact Name

_____

Phone _____Cell

_____

Guest Count _____Arrival Time

_____

Time Meal Served _____Dessert

_____

Staff Costs:

Bartender: _____ to _____ at _____ per hr.

Servers: _____ to _____ at _____ per hr.

Chef: _____ to _____ at _____ per hr.

Cost Worksheet

Food Costs:

Seasonings/Garnish _____ Ice _____

Beverages _____ Meat _____

Hors D's _____ Buy outs _____

Paper Goods _____ Equipment _____

Total Food Cost: _____

Subcontractors:

Rentals _____ Flowers _____

Music/Ent. _____ Photos _____

Total Subcontractors:

_____

Deposit Due $_____ Due by _____

Bal Due $_____Due by _____

Contract
Event Name

_____

Client Name

_____

Date of Event _____ Time

_____

Address of Event

_____

Contact Name

_____

Phone Number _____ Guest Count

_____

Price per Person $_____ Total
$_____

50% Deposit due upon booking
$_____

Balance Due _____ Amt
$_____

Cancellation and Refund Policy

Payment of fifty percent (50%) deposit shall be made at the time contract is signed. No date will be held without deposit, unless arrangements have been made with management. The balance due will be required one week prior to the event.

Customer must notify management at least 30 days in advance of cancellation or postponement to receive refund of deposit, minus any costs caterer has incurred.

Cancellations of less than 30 days will forfeit the deposit unless management is able to book another client for that date, in which 25% of deposit will be refunded.

I HAVE READ AND I UNDERSTAND THE ABOVE CONDITIONS

_____

Customers Signature

**You will want to put your Cancellations and Refund Policy on the front or back of your contract. This is probably the most important part of the contract so be certain you read it aloud to the customer and get their signature before you accept the deposit.

Small Business Association - SBA

Regional Offices

Arkansas	870-910-8063
California	213-251-7253
Colorado	303-844-2607
`Connecticut	860-251-7000
D.C.	202-606-4000
Delaware	302-571-5225
Florida	305-536-5521
Georgia	404-441-0100
Hawaii	808-522-8130
Idaho	208-334-1696
Iowa	319-236-8123
Illinois	312-886-0710
Kentucky	502-574-1143
Maine	207-782-3708
Maryland	301-722-9300
Massachusetts	617-565-5615

Michigan	810-767-6455
Minnesota	612-347-6747
Missouri	816-374-6675
Montana	406-443-0800
Nebraska	402-221-3606
Nevada	702-388-6683
New Hampshire	603-225-1400
New Jersey	973-645-3968
New Mexico	505-346-7830
New York	518-446-1118
North Dakota	701-746-5160
Ohio	216-522-7580
Oklahoma	405-601-1930
Oregon	541-553-3592
Pennsylvania	412-322-6441
Rhode Island	401-528-4688
South Carolina	843-723-1773
South Dakota	605-394-1706
Tennessee	615-963-7254

Texas	915-534-0541
Utah	801-741-4251
Virginia	703-335-2000
Vermont	802-828-4422
Washington	206-553-7317
West Virginia	304-368-0023
Wyoming	307-261-6566

Women's Business Center

202-205-6673

SBA Answer Desk

800-827-5722

If you state is not listed above, call the Answer Desk for more information.

Jennifer Williams

About the Author

Jennifer Williams was born into a family of great cooks. It was her lifelong dream to own a catering business, and in 1996, she made her dream a reality. Lacking formal training, Jennifer relied on catering books, seminars and other caterers to help her get started. Within one year, she had booked fifteen jobs and had an exclusive catering deal with a local hotel.

She has taken a break from catering to focus on her son but wrote this book as her way to keep her foot in the catering door. This is Jennifer's first book, but not her last.

Jennifer hopes to teach other aspiring caterers her techniques for success by teaching one-day seminars. She's been happily married for ten years, has a three-year-old son and enjoys cooking (of course), shopping with mom, and spending time with friends. She makes her home in Southern California.

Printed in the United States
64786LVS00006B/158

9 781403 358905